CONTENTS

WHEN IS A PLANET NOT A PLANET?

At the time of its discovery in 1930, Pluto was considered the ninth **planet** as well as the smallest and most distant known planet in our **solar system**. Since 2007, however, Pluto has been getting a lot of attention for not being a planet!

When other objects similar to Pluto in size were discovered in the outer reaches of the solar system, **astronomers** began to question if little Pluto actually qualified as a planet. In 2007, the International Astronomical Union (IAU), a group of astronomers whose job is to decide how objects in space should be labeled, or classified, made a decision. Pluto would be reclassified as a **dwarf planet**.

Since 2007, there has been a lot of discussion and disagreement among astronomers and space fans about the decision to change Pluto's classification from planet to dwarf planet. What no one disagrees about, however, is that this tiny, distant, icy world remains as fascinating to study and explore as it ever did!

Pluto

Earth

That's Out of This World!

Pluto has a diameter of just 1,430 miles (2,300 km). That means 5.5 Plutos could fit across the diameter of our home planet, Earth.

This image shows Pluto's size compared to Earth.

PLUTO
AND
OTHER DWARF PLANETS

by Ruth Owen

WINDMILL
BOOKS

New York

Published in 2014 by Windmill Books, An Imprint of Rosen Publishing
29 East 21st Street, New York, NY 10010

Produced for Windmill by Ruby Tuesday Books Ltd
Editor for Ruby Tuesday Books Ltd: Mark J. Sachner
US Editor: Joshua Shadowens
Designer: Emma Randall
Consultant: Kevin Yates, Fellow of the Royal Astronomical Society

Photo Credits:
Cover, 12 (top), 14–15, © Science Photo Library; 1, 18–19 © Superstock; 4 (bottom), 8–9, 10–11, 14, 16–17, 19, 20–21, 22 (bottom), 23 (top), 24, 26–27, 28–29 © NASA; 4–5, © European Southern Observatory; 6–7, 22–23, 25 © Shutterstock; 12 (bottom) © Public Domain.

Publisher Cataloging Data

Owen, Ruth.
Pluto and other dwarf planets / by Ruth Owen.
   p. cm. — (Explore outer space)
Includes index.
ISBN 978-1-61533-730-9 (library binding) — ISBN 978-1-61533-777-4 (pbk.) —
 ISBN 978-1-61533-778-1 (6-pack)
1. Pluto (Dwarf planet) — Juvenile literature. I. Owen, Ruth, 1967–. II. Title.
QB701.O94 2014
523.482—dc23

Manufactured in the United States of America

CPSIA Compliance Information: Batch #BS13WM: For Further Information contact Windmill Books, New York, New York at 1-866-478-0556

This artwork shows how the surface of Pluto might look. The small glowing star at the top of the picture is the Sun!

A Dwarf Planet Is Born

About 4.5 billion years ago, the Sun, Pluto, Earth, and everything in the solar system did not exist. The chemical ingredients to make a solar system did exist, however. These ingredients were floating in a vast cloud of gas and dust called a **nebula**.

Over millions and millions of years, part of the cloud began to collapse on itself. Gas and dust collected, creating a massive sphere, or ball. As the sphere rotated in space, a disk formed around the sphere from the remaining gas and dust. Pressure and extreme heat built up as the material in the sphere was pressed together by **gravity**. Finally, the pressure and heat became so great that the sphere ignited to become a new **star**. That star was our Sun!

Leftover matter from the formation of the Sun continued to spin in the disk. Over time, this matter clumped together to form planets, **moons**, objects such as **asteroids**, and dwarf planets, including little Pluto. From the moment each of these objects formed, they have been circling, or **orbiting**, the Sun.

That's Out of This World!

The solar system's eight planets are Mercury, Venus, Earth, Mars, Jupiter, Saturn, Uranus, and Neptune. For 77 years, Pluto was the ninth member of this group, but today it is a member of a different solar system club.

The birth of our Sun and solar system

Newly-formed Sun

Spinning disk of gas and dust

Venus

Mars

Saturn

Neptune

Mercury

Earth

Jupiter

Uranus

Pluto

This diagram shows the solar system's eight planets and Pluto in the order they come from the Sun. The sizes of the planets and the distances between them are not to scale.

WHAT'S WHAT IN THE SOLAR SYSTEM

Classifying the different objects in the solar system can be confusing. So here's a quick guide to what's what in the solar system.

A planet is a large, round object that orbits the Sun. A "true" planet, like Mars or Earth, is so large that it has cleared its orbit, or pathway, around the Sun.

A dwarf planet also orbits the Sun and has a rounded shape. However, because it is much smaller than a true planet, a dwarf planet is not powerful enough to clear its orbital pathway of other space objects. So a dwarf planet will be found orbiting the Sun on a pathway that it shares with many other similar objects.

A moon is a rounded object that is held in orbit by the gravity of a planet, so it forever orbits that planet. Moons can be just a few miles (km) across, or as big as a planet. For example, Jupiter's huge moon Ganymede is bigger than the planet Mercury. Ganymede can't be called a planet, though, because it is not freely orbiting the Sun, but is trapped in orbit around Jupiter.

Sun

Mars

Earth

The Moon

That's Out of This World!

Asteroids are rocky objects that can be rounded or look like lumpy potatoes. An asteroid may be as small as a car or as large as a mountain. Like the other objects in the solar system, asteroids orbit the Sun. The largest asteroid in the solar system, Ceres, is so big that in 2006 it was reclassified as a dwarf planet.

8

The solar system's eight planets are not all made in the same way. Mercury, Venus, Earth, and Mars are solid planets with a rocky surface. Jupiter, Saturn, Uranus, and Neptune are made of gases and liquids and have no solid surface.

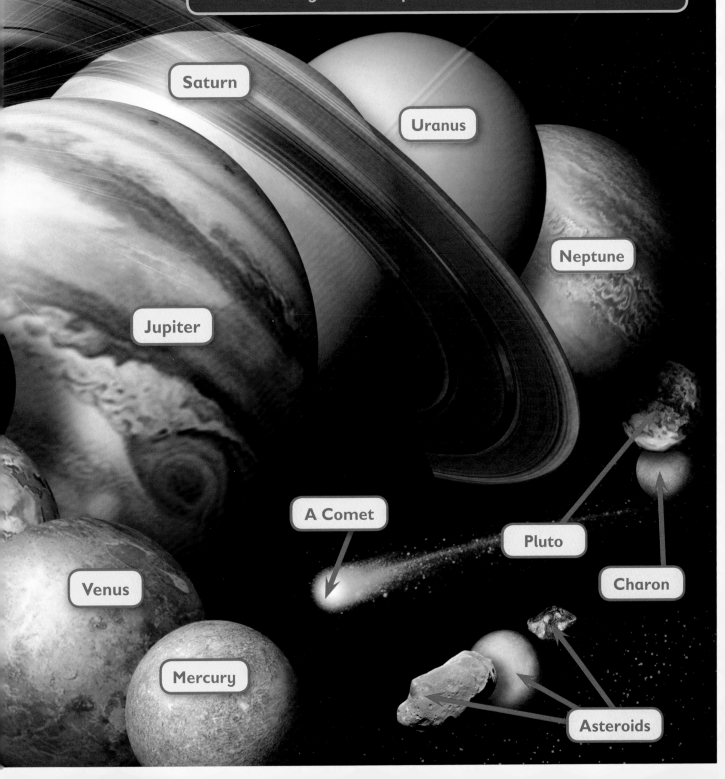

Saturn

Uranus

Neptune

Jupiter

A Comet

Pluto

Venus

Charon

Mercury

Asteroids

PLUTO'S DAYS AND YEARS

Pluto is orbiting the Sun in a region of the solar system called the Kuiper Belt. The Kuiper Belt is a region beyond the orbit of Neptune where many icy objects orbit.

Pluto is so far from the Sun that to make one full orbit, it has to travel on a journey of 22.6 billion miles (35.5 billion km). The time it takes a planet to orbit the Sun once is called a year. Earth takes 365 days to make one full orbit, so an Earth year is 365 days. Pluto needs an incredible 90,553 days, however, to make one orbit of the Sun. So a year on Pluto lasts for 248 Earth years!

Pluto's orbit around the Sun is elliptical, or oval-shaped. This means Pluto's distance from the Sun changes as it moves through its orbit. At the furthest point in its orbit, Pluto is about 4.5 billion miles (7.2 billion km) from the Sun.

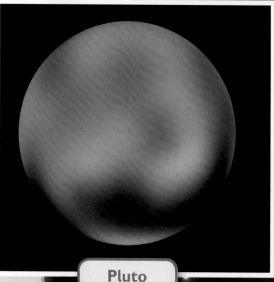

Pluto

That's Out of This World!

As each planet orbits the Sun, it also spins, or rotates, on its **axis**. Earth rotates once every 24 hours. Pluto rotates much slower than Earth and takes 153 hours to make one full rotation. Earth, Mercury, Mars, Jupiter, Saturn, and Neptune rotate in a counter-clockwise direction when viewed from above. Pluto, Venus, and Uranus rotate in a clockwise direction.

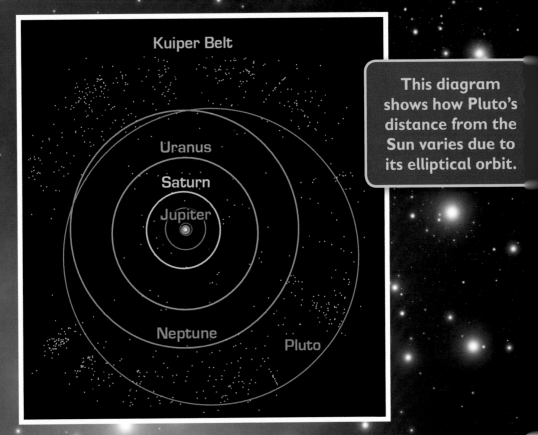

This diagram shows how Pluto's distance from the Sun varies due to its elliptical orbit.

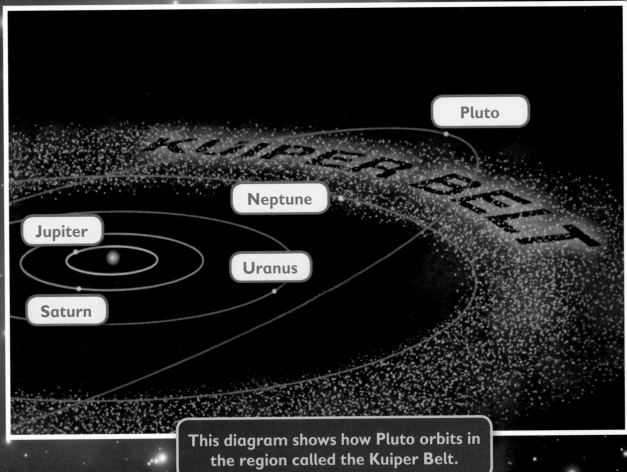

This diagram shows how Pluto orbits in the region called the Kuiper Belt.

THE DISCOVERY OF PLUTO

In the early 1900s, astronomers began searching for a ninth planet beyond Neptune.

Astronomers believed there was another body, which they called "Planet X," whose gravity was having an effect on Uranus. In 1915, this search produced two faint images of Pluto, but the astronomers who took the pictures didn't recognize what they had found.

In 1929, the Lowell Observatory, in Arizona, instructed a young American astronomer named Clyde Tombaugh to step up the search for Planet X. Tombaugh carried out his search by taking matching sets of photographs of the same area of the night sky, two weeks apart. Then he looked at the sets to see if any objects had changed their position.

Finally, in 1930, Tombaugh detected a possible moving object in one set of images. Soon, the world was introduced to what would be, for nearly 70 years, welcomed as the newest member of the solar system family of planets, Pluto.

That's Out of This World!

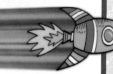

The solar system's planets are named after Roman and ancient Greek gods. Pluto was named after the Roman god of the underworld. The name Pluto was suggested by an 11-year-old British girl named Venetia Burney. Venetia's grandfather sent her suggestion to the Lowell Observatory in Arizona, and the name Pluto was selected for the newly-discovered planet.

Clyde Tombaugh uses the blink comparator equipment that he invented. The blink comparator allowed two photographs of the sky to be compared and checked for objects that had changed position.

January 23, 1930

January 29, 1930

These are the photographs that revealed a moving object that would be identified as Planet X, or Pluto. The red arrows show the difference in Pluto's position from January 23, 1930, to January 29, 1930.

Pluto, Inside and Out

Because Pluto is so far from Earth, scientists still have much to learn about this dwarf planet.

Scientists believe that Pluto has a solid core made of rock and metal. This core is surrounded by a layer called the mantle that is made up of water and ice. The hard outer crust of Pluto is made of frozen methane and nitrogen.

During times when Pluto's orbit brings it closer to the Sun, ice on the dwarf planet's surface warms and evaporates to become gas. The gases rise from the dwarf planet's surface and form an **atmosphere**. As Pluto moves further away from the Sun again, though, the gases freeze and fall back onto Pluto's surface as ice.

Pluto is very small so it only has about eight percent of the surface gravity that we experience here on Earth. This means if you weigh 100 pounds (45 kg) on Earth, you would only weigh 8 pounds (3.6 kg) on Pluto.

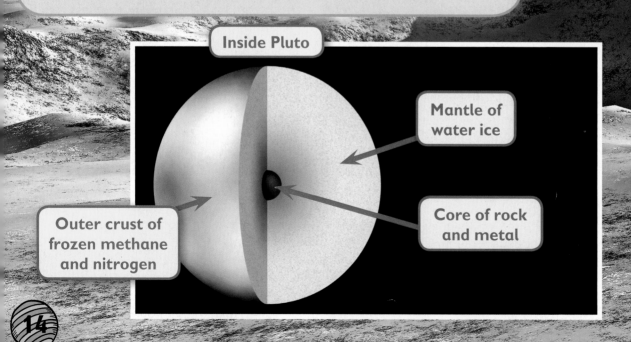

Inside Pluto

Mantle of water ice

Core of rock and metal

Outer crust of frozen methane and nitrogen

This artwork shows how the icy surface of Pluto might look. Pluto's thin atmosphere can just be seen.

Pluto's moon Charon

Atmosphere

That's Out of This World!

The maximum temperature reached on the surface of distant, icy Pluto is −369°F (−223°C).

Pluto and Charon: A Double Planet?

In 1978, American astronomer James Christy discovered what for many years was considered Pluto's only moon. It was named Charon after the mythical ferryman who carried the souls of the dead across the river Acheron into Pluto's underworld.

Charon is a small moon compared to Earth's Moon, but its diameter of about 750 miles (1,200 km) is just over half the size of Pluto's. This makes Charon actually quite a large moon compared to its "parent" planet.

When Charon was discovered, Pluto was still classified as a planet. Charon's size was so close to that of Pluto that scientists considered classifying the two bodies as a binary, or double, planet. Since Pluto was declared a dwarf planet, scientists have been discussing if the two bodies should now be considered a "dwarf double planet."

Charon is 12,200 miles (19,640 km) from Pluto. Like all moons, it is orbiting its parent body. To make one full orbit of Pluto takes Charon 6.4 days.

Pluto

Charon

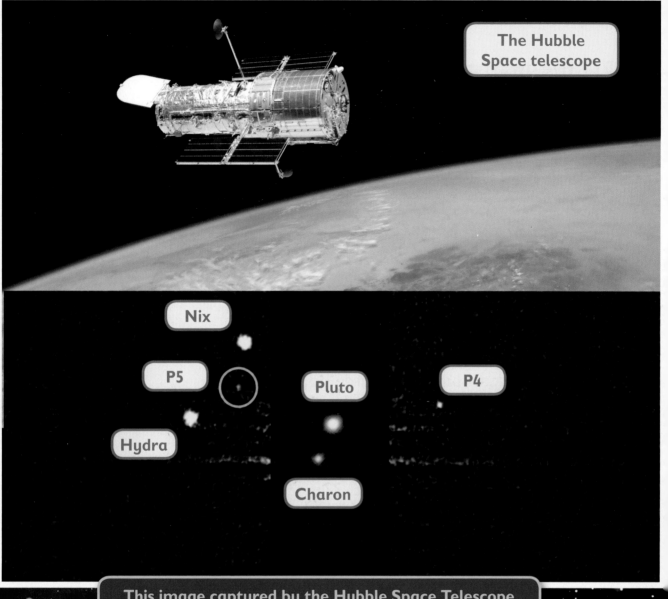

The Hubble Space telescope

Nix

P5

Pluto

P4

Hydra

Charon

This image captured by the Hubble Space Telescope shows Pluto, Charon, and the other four smaller moons.

That's Out of This World!

In 2005, the **Hubble Space Telescope** discovered two more moons orbiting Pluto. They were named Nix and Hydra. In 2011 a fourth moon was discovered, and then a fifth in 2012. The two newest moons to be discovered are tiny with diameters less than 20 miles (32 km) across. At the start of 2013, they were known only as P4 and P5 and had yet to be given official names.

OTHER DWARF PLANETS

As of 2013, five dwarf planets have been recognized by the International Astronomical Union. They are Pluto, Eris, Haumea, Makemake, and Ceres.

Like Pluto, Eris, Haumea, and Makemake are orbiting the Sun in the Kuiper Belt. Ceres, which is an asteroid and a dwarf planet, orbits much closer to the Sun, between the orbits of Mars and Jupiter, in a region known as the **asteroid belt**.

Egg-shaped Haumea is about the same size as Pluto. It is one of the fastest-spinning solar system objects yet discovered, making one full rotation on its axis every four hours! Haumea is nearly twice as wide through its **equator** than it is from one pole to the other. Scientists think that Haumea spins so rapidly on its axis that material around its equator bulges outward.

Scientists believe Makemake is slightly smaller than Pluto. This dwarf planet takes 310 years to make one full orbit of the Sun.

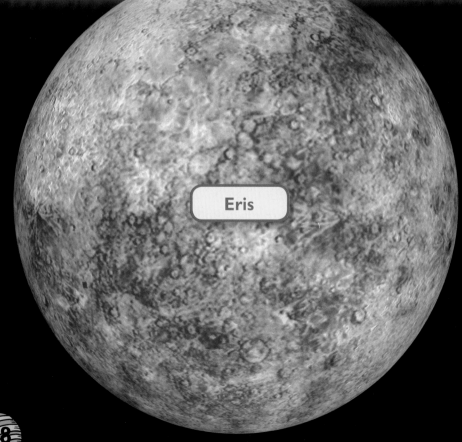

Eris

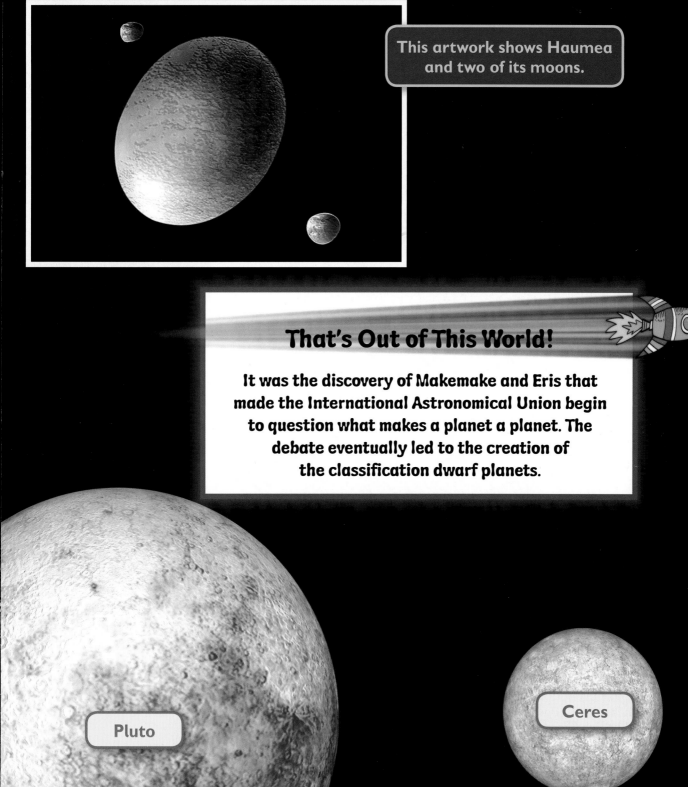

This artwork shows Haumea and two of its moons.

That's Out of This World!

It was the discovery of Makemake and Eris that made the International Astronomical Union begin to question what makes a planet a planet. The debate eventually led to the creation of the classification dwarf planets.

Pluto

Ceres

These illustrations show the sizes of Eris, Pluto, and Ceres in comparison to each other.

FOCUS ON ERIS

The dwarf planet Eris was discovered in 2005 by a team of astronomers at Palomar Observatory in California.

Eris's orbit takes it out to about three times farther from the Sun than Pluto, and nearly 97 times farther than Earth. Orbiting the Sun with Eris is its moon, Dysnomia.

Eris is so far from the Sun that it takes 557 years for it to make a single orbit. Scientists think that surface temperatures on the icy dwarf planet may only ever reach −359°F (−217°C). At first scientists thought that Eris might be larger than Pluto. Now it's believed it may be slightly smaller, but no one knows for sure. There are plenty of mysteries to be solved.

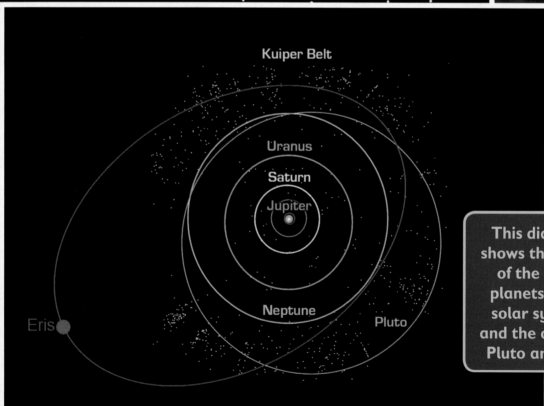

Kuiper Belt

Uranus

Saturn

Jupiter

Neptune

Pluto

Eris

This diagram shows the orbits of the outer planets of the solar system, and the orbits of Pluto and Eris.

Dysnomia

Eris

The Sun

That's Out of This World!

The team that discovered Eris initially used "Xena" as a nickname for their discovery. They took the name from the TV show *Xena: Warrior Princess*. One reason they liked this name was that it began with an "X," as in "Planet X."

CERES AND THE ASTEROID BELT

Asteroids orbit the Sun in many parts of the solar system. Today, over 500,000 have been found and studied.

Most of the solar system's asteroids are found in a huge area known as the asteroid belt. The asteroid belt is between the orbits of Mars and Jupiter. In this area, millions of asteroids form a vast, donut-shaped ring. The dwarf planet and asteroid Ceres is found in this region.

Ceres was discovered on January 1, 1801, by Italian astronomer Giuseppe Piazzi. When it was first discovered, it was classified as a planet. Some astronomers felt that Ceres was the "missing planet" between Mars and Jupiter, and it was listed as a planet in astronomy textbooks until the 1850s. The discovery of other objects in Ceres's orbit eventually led astronomers to understand, however, that Ceres wasn't a true planet. It was reclassified as an asteroid and today, it also belongs to the dwarf planet club.

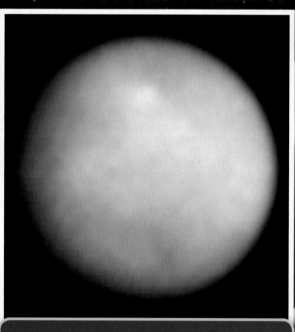

This image of Ceres was captured by the Hubble Space Telescope.

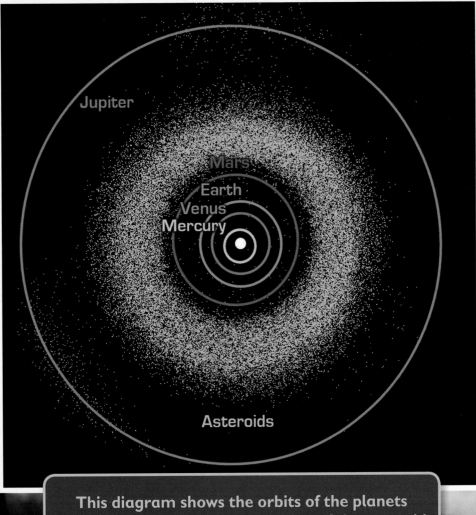

Jupiter

Mars

Earth

Venus

Mercury

Asteroids

This diagram shows the orbits of the planets closest to the Sun and the position of the asteroid belt where the dwarf planet Ceres is found.

That's Out of This World!

From its home in the asteroid belt, it takes Ceres 4.6 years to make one full orbit of the Sun.

FOCUS ON CERES

When an asteroid is discovered and its orbit has been studied and recorded, it is given a number and sometimes a name. Ceres, the first asteroid to be discovered, is officially named 1 Ceres.

Ceres was the first asteroid to be found because it was the easiest to see from Earth! Ceres has a diameter of about 600 miles (966 km), which is almost as far across as the width of Texas. It is by far the largest object in its orbital pathway, and its mass makes up between one-quarter and one-third of the total mass of the asteroid belt.

Ceres has a central core of hard, rocky material, a mantle, and a rocky outer crust. Scientists believe that the 62-mile- (100 km)-thick mantle is made up of ice. If this is correct, it would mean that Ceres contains more water than all the freshwater on Earth! Just like Earth, Ceres may also have ice at its north and south poles.

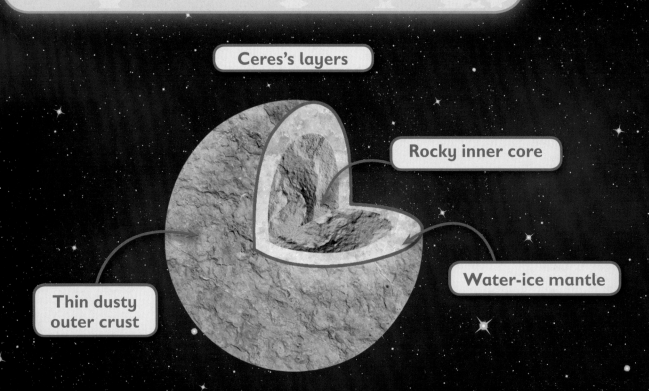

Ceres's layers

Rocky inner core

Water-ice mantle

Thin dusty outer crust

That's Out of This World!

Ceres was named for the Roman goddess
of corn and harvests.

Earth

Ceres

A size comparison
between Earth and Ceres

Exploring the Dwarf Planets

On January 19, 2006, the robotic spacecraft *New Horizons* roared into space atop an Atlas V rocket from Cape Canaveral, Florida.

If the mission is successful, *New Horizons* will be the first space probe to perform a flyby of Pluto and its five known moons. By early 2013, the craft had already flown past the orbits of Mars, Jupiter, Saturn, and Uranus. It is expected to reach Pluto by July 14, 2015.

Although *New Horizons* was still in the early stages of its journey, it created its first images of Pluto in September 2006. These pictures, taken from a distance of about 2.6 billion miles (4.2 billion km) from Pluto, were important for showing that the probe could track objects across huge distances.

This is the image of faraway Pluto captured by *New Horizons* in 2006. The arrow indicates the position of Pluto.

This is an artist's impression of *Dawn* orbiting Vesta.

That's Out of This World!

In 2007, NASA launched its *Dawn* spacecraft on a mission to the asteroid belt. There, it orbited the asteroid Vesta for over a year. Its next goal is to go into orbit around Ceres in February 2015. This will make *Dawn* the first mission to do a close-up study of a dwarf planet. *Dawn* is expected to fly as close as 430 miles (700 km) above Ceres.

THE KUIPER BELT AND BEYOND

New Horizons should fly within 6,200 miles (10,000 km) of Pluto and 17,000 miles (27,000 km) of Charon. At those close-up distances, the images of our most famous dwarf planet should be extraordinary.

Although plans haven't been finalized for *New Horizons*, the goal is to send the probe deeper into the outer solar system following its Pluto flyby. Starting in 2016, *New Horizons* will begin flybys of other objects in the Kuiper Belt, which is the home of Pluto and what may be hundreds of thousands of other objects. At the current time, the mission is scheduled to run until 2026.

The objects that *New Horizons* will study in the Kuiper Belt may include many that will eventually become classified as dwarf planets. Therefore, the *New Horizons* mission may change the way we view the make-up of our solar system for years to come.

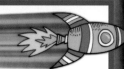
New Horizons is launched on January 19, 2006.

That's Out of This World!

As the *New Horizons* probe blasted away from Earth on its way to Pluto and beyond, it reached a speed of 36,373 miles per hour (58,536 km/h). This is the greatest speed at which a manmade object has ever been launched from Earth.

The Sun

Jupiter

Neptune

An artist's impression of *New Horizons* in the Kuiper Belt

GLOSSARY

asteroid belt (AS-teh-royd BELT) A region of the solar system between the orbits of Mars and Jupiter where the largest number of known asteroids orbit the Sun.

asteroids (AS-teh-roydz) Rocky objects orbiting the Sun and ranging in size from a few feet (m) to hundreds of miles (km) in diameter.

astronomers (uh-STRAH-nuh-merz) Scientists who specialize in the study of outer space.

atmosphere (AT-muh-sfeer) The layer of gases surrounding a planet, moon, or star.

axis (AK-sus) An imaginary line about which a body, such as a planet, rotates.

dwarf planet (DWAHRF PLA-net) An object in space that has certain characteristics that distinguishes it from other bodies orbiting the Sun. One of these is that the object be large enough and its gravity be strong enough to have caused it to become nearly round. Also, its orbit around the Sun cannot have been swept clear of other bodies, as would be the case with the larger planets, and it must not be a moon of a larger planet.

equator (ih-KWAY-tur) An imaginary line circling a body, such as a planet, which is an equal distance between its north and south poles.

gravity (GRA-vuh-tee) The force that causes objects to be attracted toward Earth's center or toward other physical bodies in space, such as stars, planets, and moons.

Hubble Space Telescope (HUH-bul SPAYS TEL-uh-skohp) A telescope that is orbiting the Earth outside of Earth's atmosphere. Unlike telescopes on Earth, it can detect distant objects in space more clearly because its view is not blurred by the gases in Earth's atmosphere.

moons (MOONZ) Natural objects that orbit a planet.

nebula (NEH-byuh-luh) A massive cloud of gas and dust in outer space. Many nebulae are formed by the collapse of stars, releasing matter that may, over millions or billions of years, clump together to form new stars.

orbiting (OR-bit-ing) Circling around another object in a curved path.

planet (PLA-net) An object in space that is of a certain size and that orbits, or circles, a star.

solar system (SOH-ler SIS-tem) The Sun and everything that orbits around it, including asteroids, meteoroids, comets, and the planets and their moons.

star (STAR) A body in space that produces its own heat and light through the release of nuclear energy created within its core.

WEBSITES

For web resources related to the subject of this book, go to: www.windmillbooks.com/weblinks and select this book's title.

READ MORE

Kaspar, Anna. *A Look at Pluto and Other Dwarf Planets.* Astronomy Now! New York: PowerKids Press, 2007.

Loewen, Nancy. *Dwarf Planets: Pluto, Charon, and Eris.* Amazing Science: Planets. Mankato, MN: Picture Windows Books, 2008.

Roza, Greg. *Pluto: The Dwarf Planet.* Our Solar System. New York: Gareth Stevens Leveled Readers, 2010.

INDEX